BOTTOMS UP

Written by GigiJack

Illustrated by Woodrat Jay

... and you turn yourself around
that's what it's all about

WGA registered 2012449 2020

All rights reserved. No part of this book may be used
or reproduced in any manner whatsoever without
written permission except in the case of brief quotations
embodied in critical articles and reviews.
Printed in the United States of America

ISBN: 978-1-7351467-0-6

Published by JackieMo Books.

In the town of Bottoms Up, the people whom you greet are walking on their hands and waving with their feet.

Mya spins her friends, round and round and round.
She pushes with her foot. Her hand is on the ground.

IT'S MOSTLY NOT A PROBLEM ...

Josephina is a bowler and brags about her score.

She points her toe in perfect form; the crowd yells out for more..

Her confidence is roaring She's quite a good athlete. She flicks the ball right off her toe, then pushes with both feet.

IT'S MOSTLY NOT A PROBLEM ...

No matter what the problems are,
I'm sure you now have guessed,
that walking on their hands all day
is what they think is best.

Then one night,
the sun had set,
the town was getting quiet ...

The men and women gathered and whispered in one place, pointing their big toe at him and laughing in his face.

For never had they been perplexed or wondered how to greet a stranger walking upside down by standing on his feet.

Big Jim just stood in silence, then gave a corner grin.
He waved his hand and turned around.

The people followed him.

He started at the merry-go-round.
He pushed it with his hand -

their noses in a crinkle,
as they strained to understand.

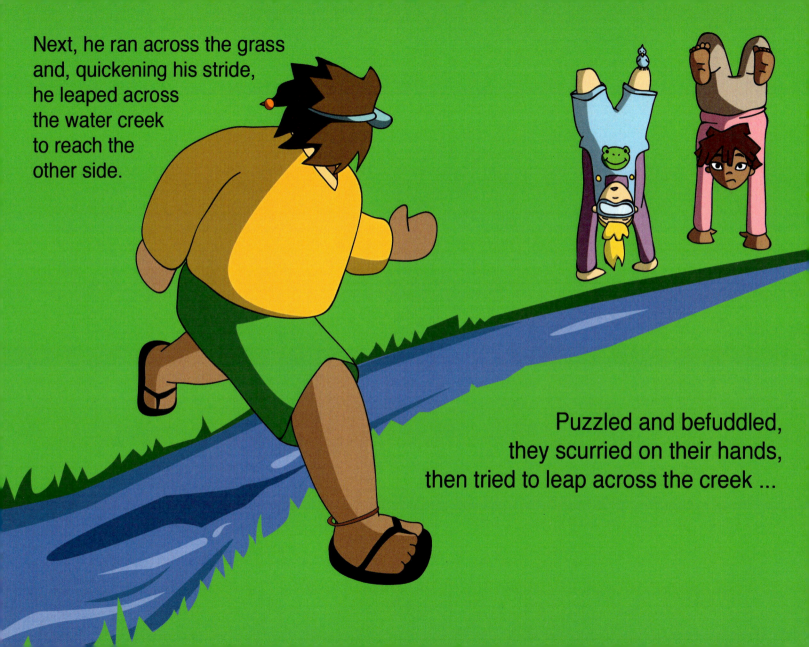

So, they gathered in a circle, eye to eye and face to face.
Like a judge without a jury, they'd put Jim in his place.
Then, with a voice of thunder, the words began to fly,
like "trickery" and "change" and "what if it's a lie!"

Some were very loud,
while others kept things in.
One thing they agreed on,
Big Jim did not fit in.

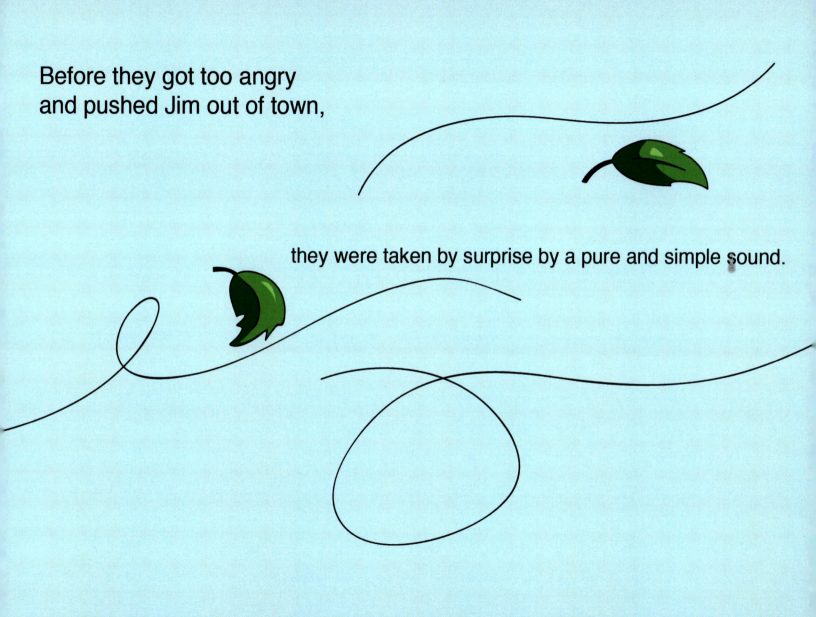

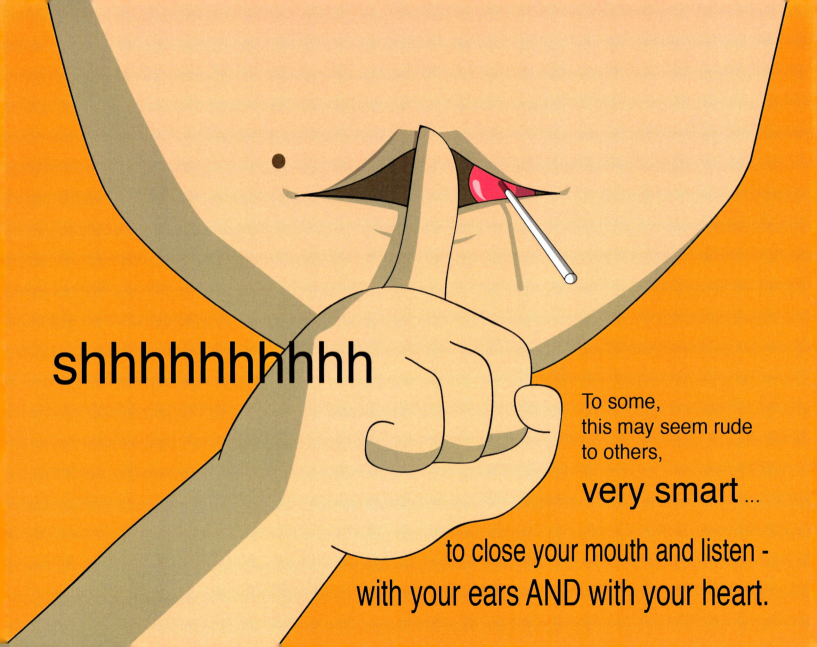

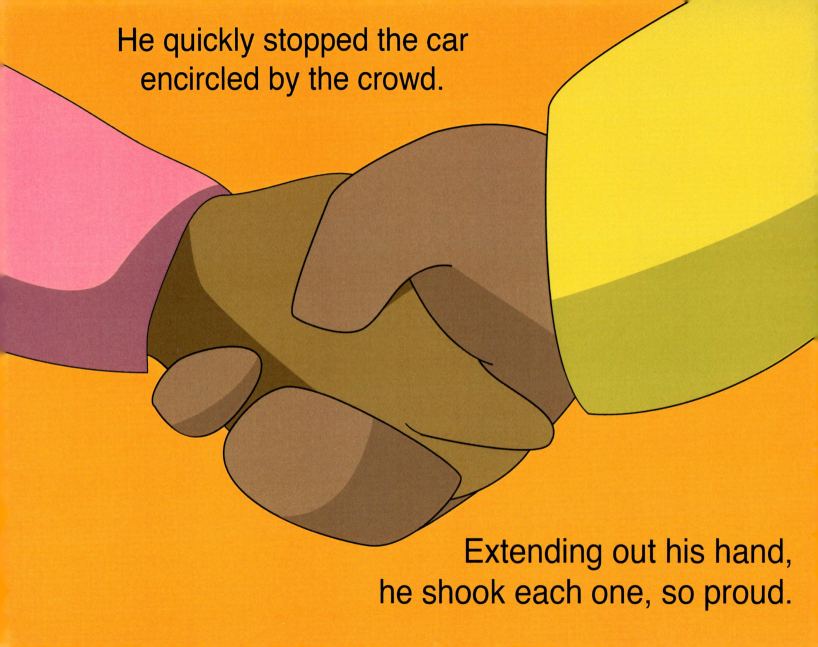

With a smile,
he tipped his hat
and hurried on his way
and with their hands,
they waved goodbye

with nothing more to say.

Learning to consider another point of view,
just might turn you all around and make you feel brand new.